Presented To:

_____

By:

_____

Date:

_____

ACKNOWLEDGEMENTS

We gratefully recognize
the work of:
Illustration Elements & Chickypooh By:
The JC Collection
Cora Artz, Editor
Copyright ©2016 by Jacqueline Charmane
The JC Collection
www.chickypooh.com

ISBN: 978-0-9974496-0-0

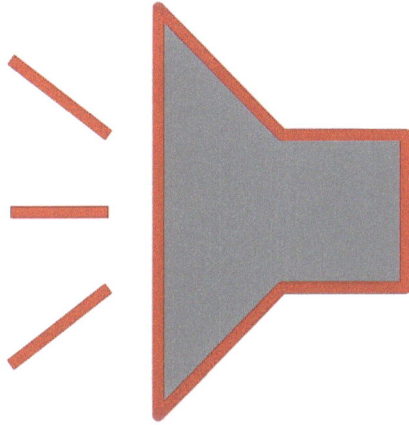

Here, Kitty, Kitty, Kitty! Is that the call of a master to a kitty? Or, is it from one who has mastered the call to the kitty?

Oh, what a shame! Oh, what a pity! That's exactly who's calling the naive little kitty.

She knows the voice of the impostor who calls her "kitty" so slick. She also knows that the call to the kitty is not a new trick.

Here, Kitty, Kitty, Kitty. Don't you hear? Master is calling you, so come near. Closer, Kitty, so that I can touch your fur. Just one touch will make you purr.

Leave her alone, said the chick with a leash on her kitty so brave. You're neither her master, nor is she your slave.

I know who I am and I'll teach her, and those like her, the same. So that they, too, will become aware of your game.

I'm warning you, impostor, back up all the way. In my very pocket is some mace I will spray.

You can't touch us because we're worth more than gold. Go away, before I scream for help, loud and bold.

See, I know how you call "here, Kitty, Kitty, Kitty," in every city. It doesn't even matter if the kitty isn't pretty.

You first make cheap offers of some measly food. From some disgusting alley-way. That's just plain rude!

For the little kitties it's soda, candy, or chips. You offer them toys, books, and colorful hair clips.

Your sick game is done. I've learned your plans. I won't be fooled with you flashing designer labels or brands.

Don't you dare take my picture with your camera, tablet, or cell phone. I've seen you lure kitties to pose in pictures then to other impostors you've shown.

HOME THEATER

EXIT

KITTY

COMING
SOON

KITTY
2

Just so you know, I'm wise, witty and wonderfully made. Your game is wacked. It's weak and already been played.

I don't care if you offer me diamonds sparkling bright. I won't give up Kitty. Not morning, noon or night.

Hiding in the shadows was a tender eyed girl with her abused kitty near. She chuckled when she heard the piercing cackles at the impostor who daily offers her beer.

"How did you get so smart?" asked the sad girl with the worn out kitty. I need help from a chick like you that is clever and witty.

Before you tell your story, let me confess about my wounded kitty. I should've taken heed of the wisdom from a woman named Old Bitty.

Old Bitty tried to tell me and show me the signs. But I wouldn't listen or pay her any mind.

I thought to myself, she's just Old Bitty. What can she tell me about taking care of my kitty?

She surely can't have one that looks as nice as mine. Her kitty has to be as old as Father Time.

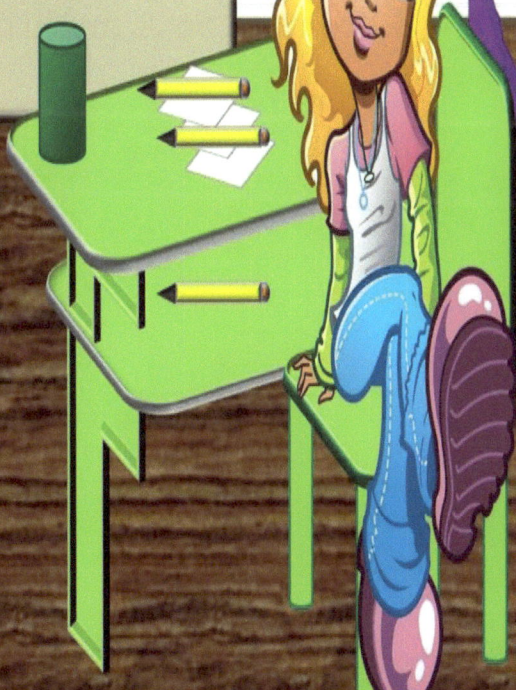

She can't have a kitty that purrs so pleasant and sweet. I bet her kitty's fur isn't at all clean or neat.

My kitty smells like roses in a springtime field. Her kitty has to look like it's missed a few meals.

Wrinkled and dried up, too old to be had. Thinking she can help me is pretty sad.

I told her that she can't teach me what I already understand. Talking to me about my kitty is like talking to the hand.

She paid me no mind because she knew I needed to be taught. No matter what I said and no matter what I thought.

She knew the impostor hoped I wouldn't listen to my teacher.
Thus, he would tell lies that were contrary to my preacher.

So, she sat me down to school me on what I've been guessing. If only I'd sincerely listened to what was deemed to be a blessing.

She said, Here's how you tell who doesn't love or respect your kitty. They will first call out your name with, "Here, Kitty, Kitty, Kitty."

No matter North, South, East, or West, when you get down to the nitty-gritty. Once you answer to the impostor's call, say goodbye to your good little kitty.

Here Kitty,

The impostor is slick
with only one purpose in
sight. That's to get your
kitty purring with all its
might.

Kitty, Kitty!

I said with a smirk to that pathetic Old Bitty, You're a country chick. What do you know about the city?

She said, no matter urban, ghetto, rural, or city, the impostor works the game without hesitation, remorse or pity.

"Here, Kitty, Kitty, Kitty," is the call, but beware not only the sound. The impostor will use whatever it takes to keep you spellbound.

Once your fur is gently stroked, your tail will slowly rise in the air. Unbeknownst to you, you're ready for the taking. You've been caught by the snare.

When it comes to protecting your kitty, here's your best defense. Don't let anyone touch your kitty. It's a capital offense.

When you're under the age of sixteen, you're protected by the law. The penalty that impostors face is more than a slap on the paw.

So, keep your kitty on a leash and out of others' beds. Your kitty is not to be touched until you wed.

The day you walk down the aisle with your chosen truelove, it's the day you get the approval and blessing from above.

I thought to myself, enough of this, you jealous Old Bitty. I can't take no more of your nagging on how to guard my kitty.

Instead I said, Yes, ma'am, knowing good and well, I had decided to show my kitty to someone who promised not to tell.

Needless to say, I should've listened to her lesson on protecting my kitty. Now, when others look at me, they say, "Hmm, what a pity."

I was only twelve when I first gave birth in some dirty litter. I stopped after fifteen when I couldn't find any sitters.

Unfortunately, at age fifteen, I had three helpless little babies conceived because of a dare. I was no longer free from care, due to the responsibilities I had to bare.

See? Here come all three, most likely hungry and wet. I even thought of giving them up for adoption to a couple I met.

But I realized it's up to me to set the best example for them to live by. Hence, I need your boldness, and most of all your wisdom, that I witnessed with my very eye.

My dream is to go back to school and get married in order to raise my babies better. They deserve a chance not to be marked with society's scarlet letter.

Oh, forgive me. They call me LayLay. Please tell me your name. I believe you can help me to be freed from the shame.

My name is Chickypooh, the chick
with a leash on her kitty. Follow me,
read my books as I tour from city
to city.

I want to teach you how to
abstain. Which means to hold back
from anything improper. Don't do it.
Refrain!

Always remember that it's never too late to do what's right. Stand firm, be strong and fight with all your might.

Today is a new day to look the impostors in the face. Say NO to ALL advances then run to a safe place.

Tell your mommy, teacher, pastor, or the police. They know how to help you make the problem cease.

Make sure you follow their instructions on staying safe from danger. They'll protect you from impostors be they a relative, a neighbor, or stranger.

Keep your head up. Don't ever quit and believe in your dreams. You can do it. Yes, you can, no matter how hard it seems.

I'll leave you a Chickypooh message to keep in mind in this and every city: Abstain from these pitfalls in life by saying NO, and keep a leash on your kitty.

About the Author

Evangelist Jacqueline Charmane is an extremely talented and gifted woman. In 1995, Jacqueline began volunteering nationally and internationally for theatrical productions. It was through freely giving of her time that her talents in theatrical productions and cultural art were cultivated. For nearly twenty years, Jacqueline has written, directed, and performed in stage plays, as well as designed spectacular costumes and dance wardrobes. As Jacqueline worked in theater, her zeal for life and laughter unfolded.

In 1998, Jacqueline began performing gospel comedy that after a decade gave rise to the character "Mother Maeye."Jacqueline (as Mother May-eye") has been seen on *Black Entertainment Television's* (BET) website, over a dozen commercials for the famous gospel talent show *"Sunday Best"* , and has two live DVD recordings. As an author, Jacqueline has written and published eight books and has plans for more. In 2010, Jacqueline branched further out in theater by founding The JC Drama Ministries and has written three plays to date. One thing is for sure, Jacqueline Charmane wisely and uniquely uses her God-given talents.

SPECIAL ACKNOWLEDGEMENTS

Illustration Characters' Contributors:
Сергей Иванов@123rf.com
Kenny Kiernan@123rf.com
Andrey Panchenko@123rf.com
blueringmedia@123rf.com
Lorelyn Medina@123rf.com
Summersun@123rf.com
Igor Zakowski@123rf.com
Teguh Mujiono@123rf.com

Chickypooh ™

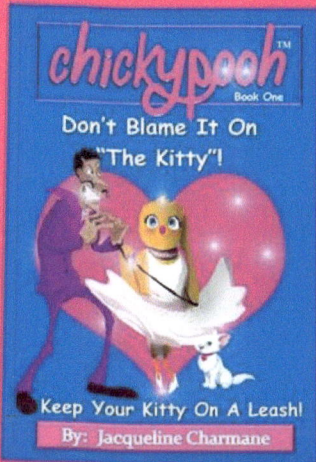

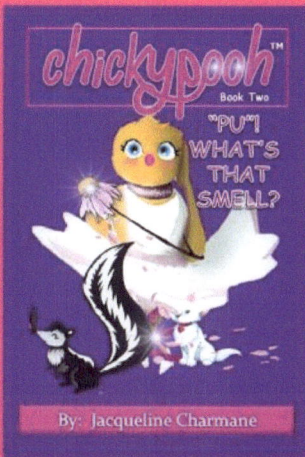

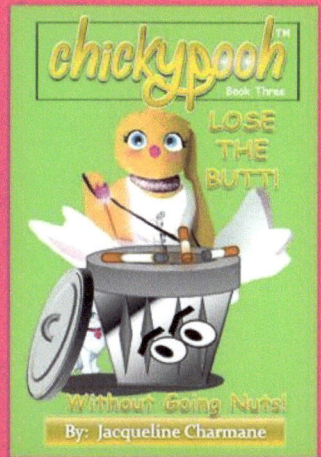

www.ingramcontent.com/pod-product-compliance
Lightning Source LLC
Chambersburg PA
CBHW040145070426
42448CB00032B/36